Ohio Violence

Previous Winners of the Vassar Miller Prize in Poetry
Scott Cairns, Founding Editor
John Poch, Series Editor

Partial Eclipse by Tony Sanders
Selected by Richard Howard

Delirium by Barbara Hamby
Selected by Cynthia Macdonald

The Sublime by Jonathan Holden
Selected by Yusef Komunyakaa

American Crawl by Paul Allen
Selected by Sydney Lea

Soul Data by Mark Svenvold
Selected by Heather McHugh

Moving & St rage by Kathy Fagan
Selected by T. R. Hummer

A Protocol for Touch by Constance Merritt
Selected by Eleanor Wilner

The Perseids by Karen Holmberg
Selected by Sherod Santos

The Self as Constellation by Jeanine Hathaway
Selected by Madeline DeFrees

Bene-Dictions by Rush Rankin
Selected by Rosanna Warren

Losing and Finding by Karen Fiser
Selected by Lynne McMahon

The Black Beach by J. T. Barbarese
Selected by Andrew Hudgins

re-entry by Michael White
Selected by Paul Mariani

The Next Settlement by Michael Robins
Selected by Anne Winters

Mister Martini by Richard Carr
Selected by Naomi Shihab Nye

Ohio Violence

poems by
Alison Stine

Flora —
Thank you for your
continued support
of my work!
Best regards

2008 Winner, Vassar Miller Prize in Poetry

University of North Texas Press
Denton, Texas

10 9 8 7 6 5 4 3 2 1

Permissions:
University of North Texas Press
1155 Union Circle #311336
Denton, TX 76203-5017

The paper used in this book meets the minimum requirements
of the American National Standard for Permanence of Paper
for Printed Library Materials, z39.48.1984. Binding materials
have been chosen for durability.

Library of Congress Cataloging-in-Publication Data

Stine, Alison, 1978–
Ohio violence : poems / by Alison Stine.
p. cm. -- (Vassar Miller prize in poetry series ; no. 16)
"2008 Winner, Vassar Miller Prize in Poetry."
ISBN 978-1-57441-258-1 (pbk. : alk. paper)
1. Ohio--Poetry. I. Title. II. Series.
PS3569.T4834O35 2009
811'.6--dc22

2008043150

Ohio Violence is Number 16 in the
Vassar Miller Prize in Poetry Series.

CONTENTS

ACKNOWLEDGMENTS

I am grateful to the editors of the following magazines, where many of the poems in this book first appeared:

32 Poems, The Antioch Review, Blackbird, Crab Orchard Review, Gulf Coast, Hayden's Ferry Review, The Journal, The Kenyon Review, Mid-American Review, New England Review, No Tell Motel, The Paris Review, Passages North, Phoebe, Pleiades, Poet Lore, Poetry, Prairie Schooner, River City, Sou'wester, Swink, and *Willow Springs.*

Some of these poems first appeared in the chapbook *Lot of My Sister* (The Kent State University Press, 2001). Reprinted with permission of The Kent State University Press.

Thank you to all my friends, colleagues, and students over the years, particularly, for their assistance with this manuscript: Maggie Anderson, Allison Armbrister, Lauren Bandman, Eavan Boland, Charlie Clark, Alice Cone, Brad Daugherty, Karen DeVinney, Katy Didden, Mike Dombrowski, Kenneth Fields, Brigit Pegeen Kelly, June Kraus, Shara Lessley, John Miller, Ander Monson, Brian Moylan, Aimee Nezhukumatathil, Eric Pankey, and John Poch. Thank you to everyone at the Wallace Stegner Fellowship at Stanford University, The Poetry Foundation, Denison University, the University of Maryland, Grand Valley State University, Gettysburg College, and the Bread Loaf Writers' Conference. Thanks especially to my family: my parents, Ashley, Andrew, James, and my husband Jordan Davis, for everything.

This book is dedicated to the memory of Paul Bennett, Richard Kraus, and Sara Medwid Gorsline.

I began in Ohio.
I still dream of home.

—James Wright

One

Fields Beyond Fields

Since we lay in the fields beyond

the high school, the boys have returned
    to claim them. The season is beginning.

Lights rasp the grass yellow.

The painted stripes shine like skin.

This is football country. We hold the coach
    higher than the clinging hands of corn.

We carry him off the field.

In this town where everyone carries

a gun against the outside, teachers spoke
    in the quiet of nicotine. Chalk clicked

like tongues. Without a pass,

I walked in halls lit as if by water.

To stop was to get caught. One hand memorized
    the closed mouths of lockers.

The gym crossed its streamers

like secrets. My fingers passed over

metal, pebbled window glass, door knobs
    numb against touch, and one, unlocked,

gave. We lay in the fields, and I

swear to you, nothing happened.

I was there. I loved him, and nothing
happened. Without our shirts,

the ground was cold and black,

full of living things that moved.

I could have touched him then, in the lightless
space between two cars on the highway.

I could have told him everything

he needed. To stop is to get caught.

The beaded tops of the wild sedge must have
tugged at his shirt, and caught

in his buttonholes, a ragged chance.

The cicadas were years from waking up,

and raising their armored heads in the long
grass to die. We lay in the fields,

our arms a last watch.

The car lights swept our bodies,

skinning us yellow, roaming over us like hands
which skim but do not touch.

ELEGY FOR THE INTERRUPTED

After the storm, the frog eggs fell.
    The rain-wash hardened to a plink.

        Small worlds burst open, gelatinous,

      each with a dotted eye, the larva curled
like a black lash. How far they came,
        ferried in the air like seeds, but seeds

who wake up in the world, lodged
    in roof tops, tire swings, trees.

        How would they ever find their way

      to water? Answer: they would find it
in a jar. When I think about my body
        formed in my mother, I think

of the order that must have been lost.
    From brain to body blooming,

        it is all about chemicals; it is always

      about them, too much or too few
inhibited, the nerves frayed,
        the blood lines blocked. At birth,

the chord can twist the neck; it can
    choke (there is something

        to be done about that), but first

there was absence: my ear done
before it was done, before the drum
　　　　learned to soak up sound and wire.

Such problems have no why,
　　　only what next. I don't think

　　　　she knew, waited, like I do,

　　　for the eggs to stir, unfurl
their feet—or not, to never move, to sit
　　　　stagnant in their trapped water.

Is it worse to act or not, to do nothing? Lack
　　　equals lack equals lacking—wait.

　　　　Send back to the brain a message:

we are through here.

CURFEW

I am late again, my body keeping its blood-store
inside my belly like a stone. What does it need
with all that blood? I have no use for a child.

I was a child. I wandered through the green wall
to neighbors' yards, my hair pinned with box
hedge leaves. My mother warned against the sky,

but I swear I did not see it change, or it changed
so quickly, gray to green like water deepened.
That summer a man wore heels, a white wig,

and walked our streets. We swore he watched us
in our sleep. From a block away, he whistled,
his light hair hardly distinct from clouds.

When they went in his house they found
rooms decorated for daughters—a red bike, a rope.
I know the difference between late and lacking.

I know what waits in me, dark spot, clinging
wire. How else was I to gauge my time, my life,
but to walk past him, turn around, then run?

Moon Lake Electric

We know our way by stars or smell,
    every collar of the gray road, every shape

        between the light switch and your corner

bed, iced in dark. Such is the course
    our bodies found, settling the hollows.

        I taught you the adaptive skills,

to watch for the eye spark of deer or dog
    along the drive. On the outskirts, we are linked

        by power, slick chords doubling

the horizon. A good marker, the sky—constant
    but for the flash of birds, and they have chosen

        to leave us. Or did we drive them away?

Moon Lake Electric pays thousands
    for the raptors found dead beneath

        their humming poles. Blackened bodies,

or sometimes, no bodies—tufts, plate bones,
    talons tight as if in the sexual helix.

        Fourteen golden eagles in one day,

and they don't know what to do with them,
    as I don't know what to do with you.

Your moods carry me as the wind

lifts feathers from the matted earth. You can
    harden me with the spiral of your skin.

      You can open me with your mouth's arrow.

Once I drove to you in a storm so thick, everything
    around me fell away. Across the bridge,

I tracked the light of trucks, then nothing.
    There's a clearing where the poles

      make angles out of air, grid the light

between road and more road. If you go, look
    for the boundary, the curl in the stratus layers—

      my body, tight as if you never

touched me, cochlear, clutching the wire. You think
    I don't know that I am the one?

      All the world does is give me signs.

OHIO VIOLENCE

By the road they leave the body. Deer,

dead deer in Ohio. *Deer Hit Special*—
   the auto shop's sign. In the grass are

      various states. Head, no head.

Tail, no tail. Neat pile only of limbs.

I learned early to differentiate. This is
   not a beast. This is part. This was once:

      the buck my brother's dog

brought up from the woods one summer,

trip by trip, a tipped hoof, leg joint. A tiny
   dog, it could only carry what it could

      carry. All summer, small burials.

The corn bled of green. You want to find

light. You want a picture. I understand.
   The story I would tell you, if you came,

      is not my story: a girl brought

her rival out to a field, and surprised her.

Watching in the rearview, the man
   they both wanted, and had. Out here,

we measure our places in blood,

bones in the weeds, the buried well.

Each brick brought a message in her
        fifteen-year-old fist. This story requires

                more telling, requires call

and response. It won't shake from me:

the lavender woods, the man—years older—
        the leaf felt and hair. Underneath my skin

                is a city. Underneath my skin

        is a crying out. You want to find light.

You want a picture. Break me open again.

THE RESCUE

He brought birds, the man from the rescue:
falcon with snipped wing; hawk with hollow
for its eye, a hole sealed over, feathers filled
in. *A man did this. A bullet.* Lead pupil,
thumb-pinched. Birds get tangled
in the wires of our telephones. Birds get
lost in our fathers' traps, and the dotted
path of our brothers' guns, and if we find
them, they are done for. To listen how he
fed them rats. To listen how the falcon
would never fly, would live its days hopping
in the leaf-spilled enclosure, straining
for rat-bits, sunning its wings. To raise our hands
when he asked for a volunteer, and then to wait
on our knees while he choose her, shaking girl,
girl in front of the classroom. He sheltered
her in leather, a rough smock. He walked
to the end of the room with his cage,
and told her to raise her hand, and told us
to close our eyes, and before we did, we saw
her waver, the thin limb extended, buffeted,
a branch. And then there was darkness,
no sound, the rush of wings only as the owl
was released. No sound as it flew above us,
no sound as it hunted mice, no sound in the room
except for the room, no sound in the night
except for the night, no sound from the owl
except when it landed, we heard the girl. That *no*.

Dream Anatomy

They've all come down at once,
    the leaves, as if this much was agreed

        upon at least, this exodus spiking

the wet grass. The trees are dark
    with balm, the soil so thick

        with minerals; here sorrel survived

a winter, frostless, each palm leaf
    spreading uneaten and deepening

        with dirt. The thyme turned in

on itself, so delicate, cast like sugar.
    In the spring I killed a snake.

        Edging the beds, heel hard

on the shovel plane, half a moon-tiled
    belly churned up, garden body

        bloodless, so neat I believed

it might heal, grow another
    like the armless earthworms. I kept

        shaking the blade, turning the pieces

over and over in the wide earth.
    But it is not spring, and the conversation

turns to dreaming, as it will,

standing between the kitchen
        and the next room, warm drinks

        abandoned. It's someone's party,

but we're not sure whose, how we
        got here, how soon we'll be leaving.

        On the threshold, a woman swears

she writes a C on her hand before sleep,
        each night in dream asking, *am I conscious?*

        Am I conscious? In my nights,

our bodies shrink and stretch.
        I would touch you except you keep

        changing. I would damp in your hands,

but your hands would pass through me—
        a slick deck, spread of tendrils, each finger

        with its own white face. If I am lucid,

then the chives. Then the basil, balled
        with blooms. If I am dreaming, then you are

        as you always are, what should

have been, what is. And is this not
        in the first person? And was I not wrong?

        Always? About everything?

When I Taught Mary to Eat Avocado

She didn't understand.

You couldn't cut straight through with the big knife
because of the pit, or heart, or stone.

We gave it many names,

and when it was revealed, bone-shade,
heavy-bottomed, she wanted to keep it.

She washed it, and the skin

dried and crackled, lost shards. I taught her to salt
in the pebbled rim, to dig with the tip

of a spoon, which is like a knife.

The flesh curl surprises, but it's a taste she'll miss.
When she stole the story I told,

how the Aztecs locked up virgins

during the avocado harvest, how this was repeated
to others in her own language,

I knew we were bound to take

what we could from each other and go.
I didn't tell her what the name

avocado meant, its connection

to the male body, which she wanted no part of,
    which I am now a part of.

       Perhaps that is the end

of the story, his flesh in my mouth. Perhaps
    the women were not locked up,

       but went in, willingly.

After the Body

Standing at the white edge where platform
stoops to track, the lowered rails, the third
one with its rush-hum, you wonder how you
made it this time, alone at night, and why,
swear you won't again. They have found
her bones in the park, scattered circuitous
by animals amid the fretted leaves, the forest
giving up its secret in layers of stench:
the heavy sweet, the vinegar. Now a slender
leg. Now a finger, a skull smashed like a star
on the spot that was once soft, that someone once,
years ago, took great care to guard. Then
the bones held something solid, live, helped her
move along the path, then shuttled through
to darkness, to the place where any one of us
could have found her, and did. On the platform,
a woman on a phone, so small she may be talking
into her own hand, paces. Now shouting. Now
rubbing her eyes. Doesn't she know people
are watching? People are staring, shuffling,
waiting for trains. You step up to the falling-off.

CHAIRS

Here is the cycle and this is what begot it:
    he touched me in cars. Nights we drove

        only to stop by the water, so still our shadows

made sounds. Light from the lake broke
    from his fingers. Once, a cruiser found us.

        I was asked if I was safe. I knew

nothing. I said *yes.* Listen: here is a story
    I never told him. In the Indiana state prison,

        the inmates made chairs. My family came

to buy, filling the back of the wagon,
    seats folded flat. I rode on my stomach

        between two crescent rockers, hewn from thick

oak and straw, glaze red as hair. With my face
    in the chair matting, I could smell the clinging sap

        rise in mist. When we slipped, it was

his scent that brought me back. How could I not
    return to him, allow the undoing

        of our clothes, his hands ascending? He came

without entering. I wanted nothing; I wanted
    to go back to the beginning. Past the prison

tower, the guards leaned into our windows

as we left, searching, cupping their hands.
    I lay in the backseat, and when he bent over me

    in the air lit by our breathing, I leaned back

so far as to see stars. The points fell on his face
    in patterns I recognized. Or made up.

    Here was the hunter, on one knee, bending.

Here was Cassiopeia—her throne, in the black light, vacant.

Not a Love Letter

Forget the moon. It is like nothing.
It is not my breast lying flat on my ribs,
not like a hand skimming water.

It is not skin, not bread. You cannot
with your mouth siphon or shape it.
That was some other moon. Some others

saw it floating, the sky a lake above
your lake. That night you showed
your land, looking like nothing in the dark:

hedges, a vague field. The garden
you had made, a ghost fence encircling
graves. The dock leaned over cloud space.

There were frogs in the shallows,
and when you circled, they dropped
each into the lake. Rain shed from the trees.

Algae flamed under feet. I think
everything I knew is ice sunk in heat.
I am trying to forget how pollen

lit your face, a chart I could follow to lip-
break, to teeth. That summer, the power
kept going out, up and down the street,

a pop of silence, like each house blew out
its porch light as each daughter came home
to sleep. I learned to dress in dimness,

cook in dimness, and in the morning,
it was salty, not sweet, the cake on my tongue;
my shirt bunched and buttoned wrong.

I am trying to forget your fingers in each
skipped space. I am trying to forget the frogs
falling one by one, their tear sound, that

sighing stone. I tell you there is no moon.
I know I have loved you only in darkness.

SCHOOL

All winter we sat blind, I next to the girl
who loved her scabs, the blood shields
her head gave up, her face a sun of blank
amazement. She drew. *This means love*:
a circle with a line through it. *More work*:
a cross. More crosses. Ice sloughed
through fields. Ice river, the pages
of our notebooks. Outside: limbs and roads
and wires. Outside cracked with force
and turning. Our poems filled with salt.
He took me to his bed.
The writer never speaks. The writer speaks
in details, the sateen lining of my coat,
the star point of tongue kissing. The winter
speaks in the whip. Run-off nixed
with ash. I spilled water on my notebook.
Words went back to ink; paper back
to ruffle, pulp. *You smell like dog*, the girl
said. You will be left like the winter.
Little sputter in the car's craw. Little
crevice in the pavement. Ice reminder.
He took me to his bed, saying: *Ali,
Ali, tell no one*. I told the girl, a sore
gathering, another skin to pick and worry.

AGAIN

Again the skin of the road is open,
    and they are shoveling tar back in.

        Tar is to take the place of the ground

after the spring. The body can horrify
    after the body. Someone has propped

        also by the road: remains of a deer,

ribboned with flesh, two legs upright,
    two set on the rail, posed as if dancing,

        and it isn't a bow at the headless,

red neck. You would know about such
    things. *Tagged,* you would call the deer,

        or call it by some other name.

And in the dark, the deer looks almost winged.
    It is brown as wings, big and leaping.

        Then dying, then dead. In the headlights,

the eyes are candied pits. Someone
    pulls out a knife. Someone pulls back

        the head. I lied when I said I could

lose you again. And again is the winter
    thinning, bark chewed through teeth,

ribs showing, but there are trees

on the other side. On the other side: the last
of the golden raspberries. Each burst

is a fingertip. Each bite is a firefly,

and again in the middle, all of the middle,
is the wet road, the star stream, the dash

amid the dashed cars, the chance,

the timing, the long long run. Run it again.
Again. I love you. I love you.

I love you. Live.

Two

The Magician's Wife

The truth is the body—his,
    bent to a sphere, unlocking

        mirror cuffs. My own, blessed

with small bones, finding
    the shape behind the false door.

        The trick is the construction,

the latching spring, the sham
    bottom, tempered by his hand.

        As a child I saw a magician

at the Hippodrome produce
    a tiger from nothing. Not

        nothing, a drawer in the set—

our seats were cheap,
    side-lighted—and I saw

        the stepping out, the answer.

He taught me how to curl
    tight, how to breathe

        in the space you are given,

arms linked in sequins.
    How to smile for the back

of the house where I once

sat, chin to velvet.
You understand how it is

to love him. You understand

I am losing a little more
of myself each night.

The saw digs a distance

from my flesh, but I feel
layers lifting, invisible,

lavender from a packed dress.

This is the trick that holds him:
my body's small enclosure.

Nothing absconds like touch,

but here, its memory
presses a shape on the bed

long after the body vanishes.

THREE

Do not mistake the sign. If you watch
    for long enough, you know. No barrel

        roll, no sheet of smoke pulled back

to show the constellation of smashed
    cars, shed gears, streaked mud. No.

        Quick, clean, Dale Earnhardt veers left,

then right, right into the wall of Daytona
    International Speedway. One hundred

        sixty thousand honeycomb the chain

link fence, and wait for him to walk away.
    He doesn't. Soon his number skulks

        on bumpers, truck cabs, T-shirts, hats.

New silence in the third turn. The fans
    raise three fingers. And in the spring,

        when a goat is born in Florida with dashes

on its black coat, the lighter fur branching
    to a figure—no one mistakes this, either.

        Three is Babe Ruth's number, but we don't

remember or want to, the number of shot
    presidents, celebrity deaths, the age

of my third grade friend's sister

when both of them died in a Lexington creek.
     For days, our parents said nothing, saved

          clippings; the baseball team walked arm

in arm through weeds. Then the girls
     were pulled out. Death made them heavy,

          hands threading roots, holding

each other. Ask me: what is it like to not know,
     then know? That sudden, that sure,

          the shaking head of the doctor come to tell

the microphone, the camera crews,
     the family, the fans—all of my stories are this

          one—all of these things are true.

Palms

Always, the faithful return to circles.
Out walking, we come across the church
at the hour they assemble into cold.
The congregation links without touching
out on the grass, their hands occupied
with light. Tonight, believers hold out
their arms for fantails: white-edged,
splintered, flat. The minister leads them,
understands they will keep what she offers,
the way the bees returned to the farm
from summer—each year, the cloud rising
from a field of dust. So when they do not
come, you will know they are dead—
disease sweeping the husks like wind
lifting the hair of a girl. Next spring,
the palms, brown and curled into fists,
will be burnt and returned to the body,
the black on each forehead, a testament
to touch, against forgetting. Will we be here
also a year, our arms cuttings? Then, a wreath.

TIRESIAS

The black snake is dead in the road.
    In the rising bands of heat, his head

        is gone, or nearly, body divided

by the flat print of tires. Already, the birds.
    I have left you and we are both

        running. What you will remember:

how the small chameleons broke
    in my clasp, blood opening like an iris

        as they fled the screen porch, shedding

cells, a slender tail. What you take
    with you now is what you know of me.

        Know everything. Know I never told you

because I wanted you to love me.
    When you came upon your parents

        in the drawn shade, the nest of their limbs

confused you. You stumbled out
    onto the porch, waking the wasps beneath

        the boards. They lit your ankle in a shower

of sparks, humming, tipped with gold.
    I know the scar like a story. Tiresias

loved as a man and woman. What was left

for him but blindness? I don't know
　　what has killed the snake as I don't know

　　　　why I killed so many, or tried to,

or thought I did. I let the scavengers
　　take what they can. I am learning

　　　　nothing has a sex. I am learning

whomever we love, we are left this way, halved.

BONES

    The bones were bones, monstrous,

magnified, like all dead waiting for wind
    or rain to reveal their sleep. What is

        beneath will always rise, unveil the chain

    end of vertebrae, the backbone's clasp,

the tail, the teeth. Such things cannot be
    brought back, only in word, given name—

        dragon—and deeds: scorched crops,

    the trees giving up their arms and returning,

solitary rods, to ash; men with blacksmith
    shields disappearing into the gash of caves,

        and girls, going always like girls do, to death

    in white gowns. All the skeletons lacked

were wings. Maybe there were wings, folded flat,
    spikes or plates smooth enough to be called

        wings, enough to fly, breathe fire, so much

    better than science which says: all the monsters

died suddenly and somehow, red haze
    shriveling plants and sanding water, the large

beasts falling, finally, starved. And we

in our crevices, stepped from the shadows, grew large.

2.
My sister the scientist says: if we live
    long enough, we all die of cancer.

        But we will not live long enough.

3.
    Then in the quickness, then in the glance?

No, I cannot find it. Perhaps the nerves, how
    the stray brought into the house still tips

        the garbage, searching still; how I look

for a lie in every pond. No, there is

nothing to suggest the dinosaur's ways:
    the belly; the legs, each a turret of meat.

        Size alone, which could not fly, which could

barely turn and meet its death—the brain,

a freckle in the blood-thick head. Even
    with studies now which say: they were

        colorful; they were sudden to spin and not

always in the water, and were striped,

and would stay with their young.
      Now the birds that gather at my feet

           have the hunger of something hunted,

     deer-brown, molting, strung with lice.

Sky rats, we call them, and they scatter
     at the slightest—the flinging hand, the car

          door opening into rain—batter

     like a beating heart after bread, only bread.

Once, bones shrunk and hollowed
     like stems. Mouths folded, hardening.

          The teeth crown shriveled. And scales

     became feathers, and claws stayed claws

but were called talons, and meat-loving
     tongues became tongues that would sing

          all night and all day until everyone

     would stop listening, forget the words,

then forget there were words at all,
     or a language, or a life before this one,

          which would never be believed.

Three

BLAME

Now you are bare inside me.
    Blood marks our movements. Let it

        line you. How it reminds you of her,

the woman you loved, the baby lost as she lay
    beneath you. There was nothing, and then

        there was. You rocked and fell out again,

and pressed between your legs like a flower,
    thin as wet paper, a beating brown sac: the boy

        in his beginning, the imprint, the ash. It was

not your fault. Everything killed the bees:
    chess-headed clovers, spring loaded with gas.

        Winter. Ice lined the combs like smoke

through the lungs. They were drawn to death,
    clotting the heart of a bull, the muscle gilded

        with stings, dripping, an asp, and then

they were drawn back out again. A virus: one
    brought it back to the others. They are like

        that. There is no right way to say this.

You were happy and tired, and I wanted to take
    both things from you, the way our clothes

fell like apples sliced from your knife, the way

the woods sighed open, each fiber, each leaf.
    I parted for you. In the field, we split the air,

        our bodies as white as the garden. What would

make the moon come down to the garden?
    Lilies and mirrors she had strung on the fence,

        feverfew, Anne's lace, to echo its light.

It was not your fault it rose, a beaten coin,
    thumb-worn, west—to turn from her flowers,

        to strike at nothing, gravel, pewter-luck grass.

She turned from her flowers, from starlight,
    from you. In the black spill of the barn,

        I was waiting. It is not my fault.

I want to go back. I want to stay standing,
    there in the field, as we were. We hung,

        not moving, just fastened: your body,

an axis; my body, a hinge—one inside the other
    upon which the world.

Fall Burning

When she brought it to him, wrapped
in paper, gray as skin and greased with rain,
his finger lay heavy on the printed word.

The news filled him with the black of broken
street lamps. The word he was following
was *ash*, a story about a fire, pollution.

She stood on the carpet, every fold of her,
rain-webbed and darkening, and it was
because of the storm that first he missed

the blood of her step. Color ran through
her hands. It took the both of them
to strip the wet layers and find its stopped

heart: a pigeon, pink-eyed, wild. Between
two cars, its wings had worked like a valve;
its mouth opened and closed, dumb.

So making love to her that night, the blood,
rust-thick, was little surprise. A red line
twisted between her legs. He stood up

from the bed, and the evidence lay heavy
as scent, a chronology of touch. He burned
the bird in a barrel with the papers and leaves

he'd been saving, slick flames beating close
to the lines. The sky flushed between two
trees. Still, the musk of smoke clung to his hands.

He buried his breath in her hair. He held
her shoulders, and his fingers made marks
where they lay—her bones, small and sharp as wings.

HOMER, OHIO

Crossing through a town between our beds, I know
we are dying like the auctioned house and the two
women farmers in Homer, Ohio. With each passing,
they fall a little further, lose the dogs, then horses.
I kiss you hard. My teeth break skin like the surface
of water, but in the morning, you forget the story
of your bruises. On my last trip, a plow for sale,
red with rain, labeled: *As is*. Women, I have seen
your sign. I am sick to death of making do. The one
I love turns from me all the while we sleep like trees,
and I know there is nothing to be born from this earth
but earth, and your scent—a gift that is turning.

In Graceland

In the garage are Cadillacs, a golf cart.
    In the yard are horses. Here it comes: another

        one about you, another one where you

are dying. I heard when Lisa Marie
    at nine found him dead or dying, marble skin

        in the bathroom, blood leadening, forehead

taking on the tub mantle, she got in her
    golf cart and circled Graceland again

        and again until the cops came. It was early

morning. It is only a story, but I think it is
    true. I think the worst thing I could have done

        is love you. No—believe you when you said

you loved, when you said: *baby, baby.*
    Your fingers that traced my collarbone were torn.

        I think of you there as if you were there,

on the bathroom floor, cold growing colder,
    growing into a museum, a chapel, a conference,

        a stamp, a black you, a Latino you, a lesbian

you. What is it about you? I have a heart
    that insists on you living, that insists on you

here and whole with black hair

and a pressed shirt, and also you old
    and fat, drugged out and hoping. And me

    in the darkness. It is me in the darkness,

and I didn't call anyone. I loved you;
    I didn't tell anyone until you were still,

    until you were found, until you were gone

from my arms and the arms of this world,
    the way you had always, already

    been, the way you have always wanted.

PORCHES

This is our work: with brushes,
    my love and I strip the porch.

        Wind-swept, the wood gives up

its winter stores. Aortic leaves,
    rot, the crumbling black earth

        go back to ground. The red mud rises,

sleek from snow. There are seven
    layers of skin; your mother was

        a nurse. I knew this already, both

things, but I was in the second stage
    of love, which is not to question.

        Think of the distance blood travels.

As we work, the black dog chases
    something under the porch.

        What thing doesn't really matter,

only that he cannot catch it,
    moors himself in the crawl space.

        You dig him free, a white towel

between his belly and snow. I know
    the place of boundary; I was there—

a woman loved you even after

losing you. Beneath skin, you carried
the trace of her, like shard

from the branch I missed,

running in new snow. I fled from a party
because they had made me

kiss a girl in a game called

suck and blow, which is played
with cards—a thin ace passed

between players by breath.

Rather than grow with the body,
the splinter in my calf softened,

shrank, a white reminder floating

between the fourth and fifth layer
like a cell between slides. It was safer

to leave it in. Understand

there are many porches. We move west
around the house, tracking the emerging

spring. The dog brings

the split earth back on his paws. We work,
not to erase, but to remember.

THE HORSE

Early morning, the broken surf,
we awake to stiffening cries.
The mare is shot in the water.
When hurt, animals recall
each other; the wounded horse becomes
the cat, then the cat-bird's wails.
All season, the banks seeded
with fish or frogs or birds in oil.
Now a bullet lodges in a horse's
throat, near bloodless, neat as an egg.
There is a kind of shocked green
this spring, as if the forsythia,
past its bloom, sprung from a chemical
pool. Or if the azaleas, not content
with purple, white, mauve,
formed a fourth petal, bright
with rain. A rancher lets his horses
loose, knowing next year they will
bring back friends. He will double
his herd, brand every one: a mouth,
his mark in the neck.

PERFECT

People are out remarking on change,
    the yellow house paint, the blue

        steps. They stop the boy slinging

color and say, *perfect*. Because it looks
    real. Because it's historic, how it might

        have been, how it was, though the other

house, the one next door, is maybe
    more real, the one that hasn't been

        touched in years, is losing itself bit

by bit, faster than the leaves, which are
    flaking now in remarkable numbers.

        Everything is remarkable, the not-so

distant purr: cicadas or crickets or birds—
    it doesn't matter. What matters is the way

        sound builds, then breaks away

as if warming up for something bigger.
    The sky cracks open. Even the boy

        is slender and naked—or nearly, enough,

his bare chest knifed with paint.
    And if a curtain rises, tacked on the point

of a broken pane, if a woman

inside shouts to the boy, if there's a radio
    to radio, so be it. You have to think of it

        as a journey, he said when he played

the tape of his time in Europe,
    the transactions, instructions, loudspeakers,

        trains. It seemed like everyone was calling

in water, but really it was the tape
    in his pocket picking up lint sounds,

        hair sounds, walking, the sound

of his penis brushed against trousers,
    the last bit of reel recording and turning—

        and then it was perfect, and then it was over.

MORPHOLOGY

What tongue or touch could last
a lazy four hours, spinning on the skin
the way a fever might? Oh subtle heat.
Oh rash brought to crest. I sat next
to you, and from your arm, I felt
a radiance, a warm tune rising
from your blood. But no, it is the bee
still secreting its fervor-haze, sting
which sticks, toxin which gums
each tip of hair, abandoned
along with abdomen, nerve ganglion,
muscles—all these parts the bee
gives up from its body. And why?
Only to make more hurt, as I do,
waiting for the lover to love me first.
Everything's a sign, or nothing is.
The sting works, bottomless, pulsing
with grooves. Valve and piston
pump venom from sac. Oh barb.
Oh anchor of traction: insist,
then finish. The wound grows
large. The dead bee still threads
poison which must be sucked,
otherwise it stays. Do you know
what I would say to you?
Go deeper.

SWIMMER

The water's dark where it is
    deepest, straight and streaked

       with heat. In the middle,

rocks wait. Clothes puddle where they fell,
    cast aside by swimmers, jeans

       and shirts in two piles, a hole

in the middle where the body
    went, fit like a slender column.

       When you died, they said *slipped.*

They said *head*, and they said
    breath. There was something

       about your breath;

you could not wake to save yourself.
    The current pushed like muscles,

       sent you down and back again,

buoyed in the white waves.
    We swore we saw so much

       in woods, in water, and we did.

Once, a copperhead skimmed
    the shallows as we swam.

We waited on rocks till night fell.

Our parents came to us in boats.
    Scanning the surface, I can see

        nothing, no trace, no limb lifted

in stroke, the flash of a head
    turning to breathe. Only

        the clothes, the cast-off skin.

On the far shore, ripples rise
    and swell into the enviable dark.

Everything Is an Instrument

Animals in the dark are approaching the house
    in waves they must have worked out.

        She watches them from the kitchen.

The light around her falls like cloth.
    The ground falls away from the house

        in back, from the rabbits; raccoons;

her family's goats, which her uncles as boys
    had named *Dad* and *Sunshine*. Holes

        in the earth, wide enough for a fist.

The dead speak through the radio
    and the grocery store clerk, who, in his

        handling of coin and bill, says: *Go out*

there and do good, and it seems as if he is
    speaking from a long way off, like the words

        have come from a river and not his nicked-

from-shaving-mouth. Out there men say: she heard
    what she wanted to hear, and the street

        lights snapped off after she passed

because they were going to anyway. But listen,
    there were also the animals, and no one

has said anything about the animals, the way,

after the girls died, deer came from the woods.
It was late. Deer gathered on the patio

as if there was a party, taking from the rose

and verbena small doses, and they were heavy
with young, which branched and bubbled

inside them like yeast, would grow heads,

then horns. Then there would be others
to also come with coin-clicking tongues,

to offer, then swallow, her only way home.

When the Hand Is a Knife

Does it matter if it didn't happen?
All day I watch my students
play in the graveyard. One girl
lies down for her friend's photographs,
fanning her hair over her breast as if
in a magazine-fold. Did the officer
say to her, as to me: *I don't know
means yes*, and did the nurse's light,
cast through her legs, shine clear
to the bell-tongue of her mouth?
We don't ask truth of fiction, and I
wouldn't ask my class, instead: *say
the narrator, not you*. Because it
might not be you. Because it might
have happened differently, or to
someone else. How then to explain
the hand, the memory of touch?
Like soapstone, a lava slice, dry-hard,
spilt, stretching to a maw the neck
of the dress I would not wear again.
Believe me. I am telling you a story.

CATALOGUE

Everything reminds me of something else.
    The last snow on the roof is a skirt,

        an arm, a lip under teeth.

I tried to remember your scent as your own,
    and not as peppermint left in a pocket,

        a leather coat, a haze I could walk through

and be taken back to Mansfield, to grade school,
    to a market in which I bought a jacket

        after haggling over stains. It was more

than you, more than essence splashed
    in haste as you shaved, as you pulled on

        your clothes. And my own scent, vanilla,

ruminative of home—kitchen, cinnamon.
    I wore it to take you back home, or

        thought to. The more we tell a story

the more it becomes what we want it to be.
    What I wanted to be was singular, a girl,

        not a city, not a day in April when you lost

your hat in a cab, when you chased after it,
    or tried to, with half a heart, your hand

on the trunk as it hopped the curb.

In this way you are not yourself. In this way
    you are my last love and the love before,

        and the next one I will mistake for you,

will want because I want you still. I will look
    for you in him, and I am thinking of the bat

        which found its way to my room,

all night hanging like a moon from the shade
    until morning; you worked up your nerve.

        You shut it up in a white towel. So light,

you said. Barely a breath. You threw
    the towel out the open door. In arc, the bat

        untangled itself, found its wings, found flight.

In the air it became more than itself. In the air
    it became an archway, a viaduct, a hook

        and eye, a kite, until finally, it was a child,

riding his bike in the street, hard and fast,
    his hands off the bars, his eyes straight ahead,

        red shirt billowing out behind.

White Fence

These nights I think I know what the world wants.
Mostly, an ending: the glaciers awake, harbors

turned to meadows. But you, you were different,
alert at the edge, awaiting some direction. We seek

death because we are strange to it. Mostly I imagine
you riding your bicycle into the trees, as far as you

could, until dead wood. What was it you were
seeking? The forest's center stillness, more limbs

on the ground than in air? Other times I think
I told you to go, turning to the light to see what fell there.

Nothing, then the whitest wing, water moths of snow
which clung to trees until the trees thinned, half

in shadow, half gone, in this way like acid. This then
is your gift to me: distance, a white fence. Ask yourself,

is this what you wanted? Go on. Ask me anything.

In the Limbo of Lost Toys

Someone stole his sister's best
    and speared them on street signs,

        lamp posts, poles, in celebration

of the school year's end.
    A lion bisected by a stop sign,

        the straw ticking of his insides

spilled, a doll with x's
    in her eyes. The plush

        kingdom softened, lost to rain.

Some of these I took. Some
    were taken back, and it was

        celebratory, like it is now

when the spoils were once alive,
    pausing in their winter pick

        of bark and lower branches.

Now the deer have open eyes,
    and whatever dreams they have

        are dreams disturbed by highway

winds, lashed to truck hoods.
    I am told not to look, but look.

How still the dead. How you

are dead, and dead, I might
        liken you to the toy horse, drowned

                in the fish pool, the way all toys

meet violent ends, legs crossed
        in axis, eyes full of milk. I might

                liken you to hunters who are

waking up only to lie again
        in mold-black trees, so still

                as to pass for always. In truth,

nothing will scare the deer,
        not even death: unreadable,

                roped to bike racks. I might

liken you to everything I lost:
        the white dog disappearing

                in a storm, and later, the black

running into hacked-off fields
        behind which waited flushing

                birds, new families. But then

I am forever linking things
        to animals. All this I lost

before I lost you, and like you,

all of it changed under new snow,
    rain which cored finger-wide

    holes, the first grass rolling out

wet and curled from inside
    your eyes, which are wider now

    but not surprised.

Praise for Previous Winners of the
Vassar Miller Prize in Poetry

Mister Martini
"This is a truly original book. There's nothing extra: sharp and clear and astonishing. Viva!"—Naomi Shihab Nye, author of *Fuel*, judge

The Next Settlement:
"Michael Robins' prismatic poems open windows, then close them, so we're always getting glimpses of light that suggest a larger world. With never a syllable to spare, these poems are beautiful and haunting. I know of nothing like them."—James Tate, winner of the 1992 Pulitzer Prize for Poetry

"*The Next Settlement* is a finely honed, resonant collection of poems, sharp and vivid in language, uncompromising in judgment. The voice in this book is unsparing, often distressed, and involved in a world which is intrusive, violent, and deeply deceitful, where honesty and compassion are sought for in vain, and refuges for the mind are rare." —Anne Winters, author of *The Key to the City*, judge

re-entry:
"Michael White's third volume does what all good poetry does: it presents the sun-drenched quotidiana of our lives, and lifts it all into the sacred space of poetry and memory. He delights us with his naming, but he also makes us pause, long enough at least to take very careful stock of what we have. He makes us want to hold on to it, even as it trembles in the ether and dissolves."—Paul Mariani, author of *Deaths and Transfigurations*, judge

"Here is a book that explores the interplay between interior and exterior landscapes with such generous and beautifully crafted detail that readers will feel they are no longer reading these poems but living them." —Kathryn Stripling Byer, Poet Laureate of North Carolina

"In Michael White's latest opus, figure after figure emerge from chaotic ground of memory, such verdant upswellings an urgent music pressured up from deep wells before subsiding—high waterlines left in our wake to mark the turbulence of love's intractable flood." —Timothy Liu, author of *For Dust Thou Art*

The Black Beach:
"*The Black Beach* constantly delights with its questing, surprising, and not-easily-satisfied imagination. But simultaneously it creates an exacting and exhilarating vision of 'God, the undoer that does.' The speaker who, in one poem, stands in the moment 'love/what is not,' is the same one who, in another poem, imagines 'the black beach of heaven where all desire/ is merged, twinned, recovered, braided, and set ablaze.'" —Andrew Hudgins, author of *Ecstatic in the Poison*, judge

"A dark brilliance shines in these honed, memorable poems of the human predicament: that of a sentient particle with a mind for the infinite. 'Looking for meaning/ the way radio waves sought Marconi,' Barbarese's restless imagination searches through the stations of the daily to the 'very end of the dial/ the static that never signs off,' and turns back to receive what we have, the 'lonely surprised heart/ shaken. . .'" —Eleanor Wilner, author of *The Girl with Bees in Her Hair*

"Barbarese has an uncanny ability to size up the urban scene, then hallow and harrow it. Putting his daughter on the local train for the city, he conjures up those who rode in the boxcars to the ovens. And, leaning over 'winged rot . . . glued . . . to shat-on grass' in a nearby park, he can think 'how beautiful,/ the hard frost had cemented/ what had lived to what never did.' He wins me over in poem after poem."—Maxine Kumin, author of *The Long Marriage*

Losing and Finding:
"There are so many delights in this book, interpenetrated by so many losses. . . . She keeps her eye unflinchingly on 'the rough loving arms of this world,' even as she is buffeted about by it."—Lynne McMahon, Judge

"From the searing heart of pain and patience come the transporting poems of Karen Fiser. Trust them. Treasure them. These poems are resounding, important, and deeply humane."—Naomi Shihab Nye, author of *Fuel*

Bene-Dictions:
"*Bene-Dictions* is a canny, unnerving book. Its cool manners seem to hold compassion at bay; but its irony is a cleansing discipline which allows it to conjure complex lusts, hurts, and injustices without self-pity and, apparently, without delusion. These poems describe a world in which 'Tenderness is an accident of character/ or energy, or just a side-effect/ of having failed at what you wanted,' but in which the reader, to read the effect of rain on paper, 'opens the book/ in a storm, as though to find the world itself in tears.'"—Rosanna Warren, judge

"If the long hours in offices of the mind elect for us meaningfulness, they must always eventually find the human heart. Then Rankin's vivid and surprising poems map that movement where as Rilke insists, what is sublime is mundane, and everything that falls must somehow in shadow/act, rise."—Norman Dubie

Self as Constellation:
"This is a collection to be read in sequence because the continuity is powerful and persuasive. If we are attentive readers, we end like the nuns in the storm cellar 'not knowing whether we've been struck by lightning or by love.'"–Madeline DeFrees, judge

Perseids:
"It is a rare pleasure to encounter these days a young poet so thoroughly at home in the natural world, so deeply attuned to its mysteries, that reading her book we enter, in turn, that 'Spherical Mirror,' the elemental mind which, as *The Perseids* reminds us, forms 'the core of human bliss.'"—Sherod Santos, judge

Protocol for Touch
"Merritt's prosodic range is prodigious—she moves in poetic forms as naturally as a body moves in its skin, even as her lines ring with the cadenced authority of a gifted and schooled ear. Here, in her words, the

iambic ground bass is in its vital questioning mode: 'The heart's insistent undersong: how live? // how live? How live?' this poetry serves no lesser necessity than to ask that."—Eleanor Wilner, judge and author of *The Girl with Bees in Her Hair*

Moving & St rage

"Kathy Fagan's long awaited second collection keeps revealing new strengths, new powers. Its words are of unsparing rigor; its intelligence and vision continually spring forward in changed ways. These are poems both revealing and resistant: deeply felt, deeply communicative, yet avoiding any easy lyricism. Again and again the reader pauses, astonished by some fresh turn of language, of insight, of terrain. *Moving & St rage* offers extraordinary pleasures, clarities, and depth."—Jane Hirshfield

"From the first emblems of language—the angular letters of A and K—a child steps toward the preservation of consciousness, and, in turn, the paradox of preserving that which is lost. These beautifully crafted poems trace a journey to adulthood and grief with a lyrical mastery that is breathtaking. *What can language do with loss?* Fagan asks. This splendid book is her answer."—Linda Bierds

Soul Data

"*Soul Data* is rarely compounded—of wit and music, surface elegance and intellectual depth, quirk and quandary. Its sensual intelligence is on high alert, and the sheer unsheerness of its language—all its densities and textures—is a linguiphiliacal delight. Unmistakably American (the poetry's occasions and its cadences alike serve for signature) it has the jinx-meister's humors about it. A fine rhetorical savvy, in a mind inclined to the chillier depths: among poetic gifts these days it's an uncommon conjunction, a gift of mysteries, like the sight (across a night pond's surface) of bright-blue shooting star: one hopes the other humans get to see it."—Heather McHugh

American Crawl

"It is absolutely no exaggeration to say that no one is writing like Paul Allen. There is not an ounce of flab in his poems, which are informed by an urgency, a sense of personal commitment, and a passion rarely seen in contemporary poetry. America in the 1990s is not a comfortable world in which to live; and Paul Allen is certainly not the man to entertain us with fanciful invitations to dens of innocence. Though *American Crawl* is a first book, there is nothing jejune about the poems, or about the unique imagination that creates them. The publication of this book is an important contribution to American letters."—Richard Tillinghast, author of *The New Life*

The Sublime

"*The Sublime* embodies a poetry that is personal and public, and shows through clear-cut imagery how varied our imagined and actual lives are. Everything seems to be woven into this ambitious collection: love, war, divorce, fear, anger, doubt, grace, beauty, terror, popular culture, nature. This poetry challenges us to remain (or become) whole in an increasingly fragmented world."–Yusef Komunyakaa, judge

Delirium

"Barbara Hamby is an extraordinary discovery! A poet of compassion and elegance, she is a poet whose debut in *Delirium* promises a rich (and enriching) lifelong project."—Cynthia Macdonald

Partial Eclipse:

"Sanders brings together his own sensibility (quizzical, approaching middle-age, slightly disaffected, bemused, learned but not stuffy) and an alertness to what can be appropriated from history, myth, the daily papers."— *Choice*

". . . a distinguished first collection from a poet about whom we will be hearing more."— *Houston Post*

"Sanders proceeds through his . . . poems with a pervasive steadiness of diction, . . . a syntactic resonance quite his own yet gratefully beholden to such exacting masters as Stevens and Ashbery. The freshness of the poems is a result of their immersion in life with others, achieving the resolute tonality of a man speaking not so much out or up but on, talking his way to the horizon."—Richard Howard, judge